BEAUTY AND THE BEAST

(As performed by ARIANA GRANDE and JOHN LEGEND)

Disney

Beauty
AND THE
Beast

Music by ALAN MENKEN
Lyrics by HOWARD ASHMAN

BEAUTY AND THE BEAST

(As performed by Ariana Grande and John Legend)

from BEAUTY AND THE BEAST

Music by ALAN MENKEN
Lyrics by HOWARD ASHMAN

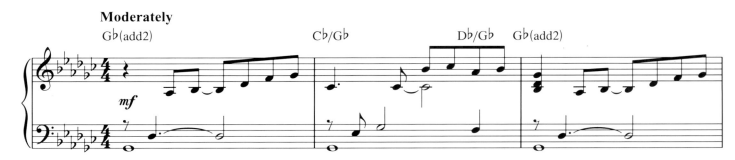

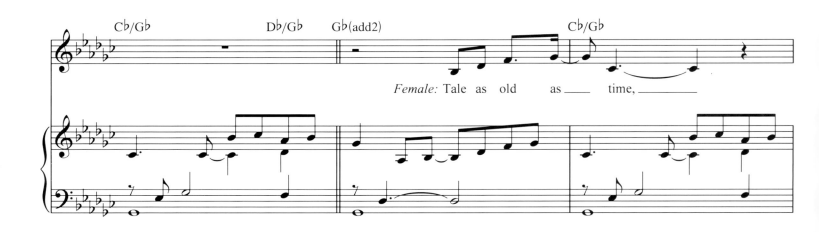

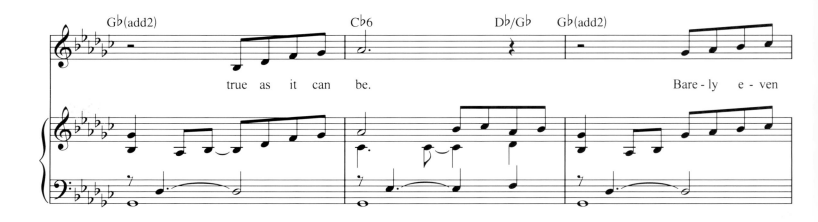

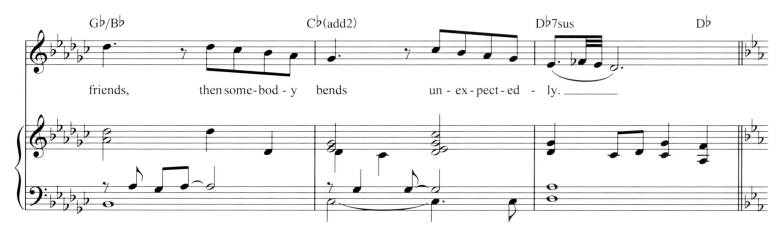

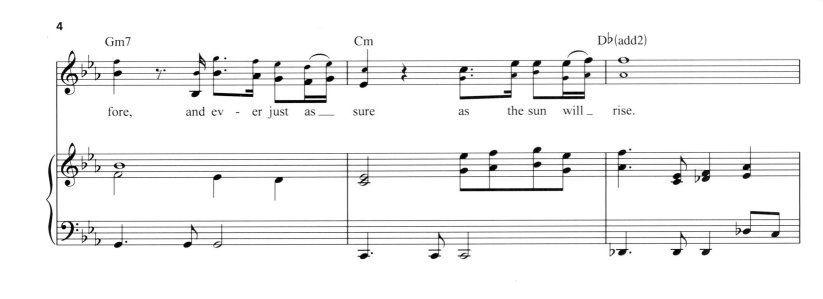

fore, and ev - er just as __ sure as the sun will __ rise.

Lead vocals ad lib.

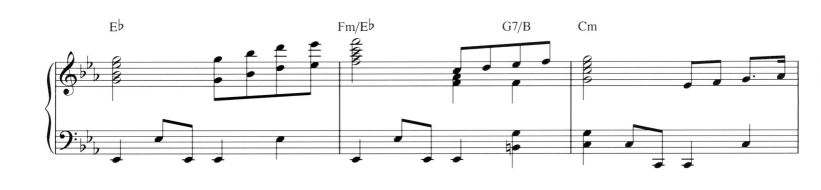

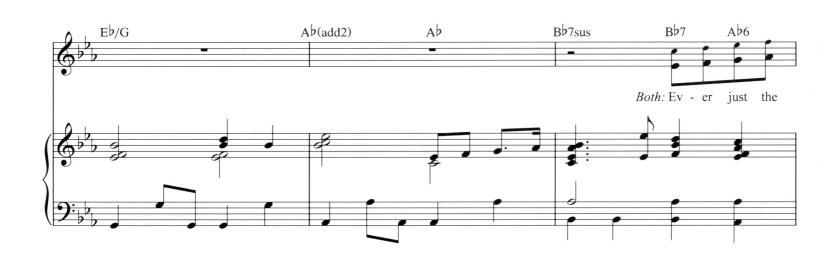

Both: Ev - er just the

WONDERLAND MUSIC COMPANY, INC.
WALT DISNEY MUSIC COMPANY

DISTRIBUTED BY

7777 W. BLUEMOUND RD. P.O. BOX 13819 MILWAUKEE, WI 53213

To access companion recorded accompaniment online, visit:
www.halleonard.com/mylibrary
Enter Code
1372-1085-4824-1134

ISBN 978-1-4950-9526-9

9 781495 095269